Just Say "Hi"™

to

Amazing
PARTS
of
YourSELF

Is It *DID* ...or Just Parts of Me?

Julie Kalmenson Lyons, LICSW

Just Say "Hi"™ to Amazing Parts of Yourself
Is It *DID* … Or Just Parts of Me?
by Julie Kalmenson Lyons, LICSW
https://www.justsay-hi.com/
https://www.aboldstep.org/

ISBN-paperback: 978-1-952281-53-2
ISBN-eBook: 978-1-952281-54-9

Endorsements

"Julie Lyons has shown me pathways to self-discovery I never knew existed. Done with love, compassion, and empathy."

Gary Stromberg
Film Producer/Former PR Manager for *The Rolling Stones*/Author of *The Harder They Fall*

"Julie Lyons knows what she's talking about. She's earned the right to talk about recovery from *DID* from her own experience and by helping others having difficulty dealing with their uniqueness. She has come up with a clever method, not only to reduce one's suffering, but to turn what we thought were handicaps into assets."

Lewis Teague
Film Director, *The Jewel of the Nile*

"Reading Julie's book has helped me to be more mindful of language and to sharpen my tools to help communicate with my musician colleagues, friends, wife, kids, and family. Reframing labeling folks with mental illness to embracing a rainbow of mental diversity! Julie certainly offers tools for every person, as all of us have aspects of ourselves that when we discover them, we discover what holds the keys to our own uniqueness, skill set, and genius!"

Nick Russo, B.S., M.A
NYC Musician/Educator, aka "Banjo Nickaru" of *The Scooches*

"Challenges...we all face them. Many people stay in a cycle of grief, denying the truth of who they are. *Just Say 'Hi'* demonstrates a new playful way to embrace all aspects of yourself."

**Dr. Birgitte Tan, Transformational Life &
Grief Recovery Coach
Creator of *Joyful Riches Beyond Grief* ®,
Author of *Seeking Peace***

"*Just Say 'Hi'* is a book not only for people with *DID*, but really for anyone and everyone looking for a way to embrace all of themselves. It is written with compassion and understanding, from someone who understands. Julie has dedicated decades to the study of multiple identities, and she shares her expertise in a tested method that can get anyone to better harmonize with aspects of themselves that need love and attention. Really anyone can benefit from this book. I thoroughly enjoyed reading it and recommend it for everyone."

**Serena Sun
Coach, Creative, Teacher, Founder of the mental health organization *Breaking Taboo*.**

"Julie Lyons presents an inclusive and modern way to look at diverse characteristics and coping styles. She encourages us all to embrace human differences with curiosity; to work with the parts of ourselves instead of against them and each other. This handbook is easy to understand and moves you forward in your life; it's how to get unstuck without the typical self-help or therapy talk."

**Patrick Snow, Book/Publishing Coach
International Best-Selling Author of *Creating Your Own Destiny***

"Julie has found a light-hearted way to help us connect with internal parts of ourselves, especially when those parts may be at odds. The end result is feeling good. I immediately applied these concepts to my work as a Guardian ad Litem to connect with the children I serve."

Dee Gretzler
Guardian ad Litem

"After reading the book, I closed my eyes and felt my inner child come to me and give me a hug. I asked, "How can I help?" She said she was OK; she just wanted a hug (like the ones my son gives, for no reason, just because, why not?). It brought tears to my eyes. This is big; I don't think I ever had this experience in a guided meditation or as a child. Thank you, Julie. I made sure I thanked my inner child too. It was lovely. I'm amazed at how simple and effective it is.
I will keep using it. Beautiful work."

Angelica Swanson
Full-time Mother/Student

Dedication:

To Benjamin Blackett
for providing me the opportunity
to meet my mentor,
Mary Morrissey
(and the Brave Thinking Institute family),
who taught me how to love, so I could love
my own mother and she could love me
before she passed on December 31, 2020

And
to my good friend
Leonard "Lenny" Lake
who always called
to

Just Say "Hi"™

Also...

To the courageous clients I have
had the honor to serve and
all who have fought for
diversity, equality, freedom,
and safety for others
to

Just Be Who We Are

Acknowledgments

Serena Sun for coaching me to move beyond my
own stuckness;
Patrick Snow for encouraging me to write, speak,
and publish my work;
Melissa Marcello for always believing in my
dreams;
Michael Barron for walking the walk with me,
helping me find joy, sometimes through
puddles of tears;
Esme Hecht for unconditional love and support;
Valerie Carrington and her mom, Maria, for
helping me follow my heart;
Birgitte Tan, Dee Gretzler, and Tawny Solmere for
their deep commitment to friendship and
growing together no matter where we are;
Harvey Kalmenson, my dad, for helping to make
me the woman I am; Cathy Kalmenson for the
woman you are;
and
Ellen Kalmenson for being a great sister

Foreword

Julie Kalmenson Lyons knows from personal experience what it's like to be labeled, stigmatized, and stuck. Her life circumstances led to developing symptoms of a mental health condition believed to be rare and untreatable, but Julie refused to let that get in her way.

In the book *Just Say "Hi,"*™ Julie shows you how to acknowledge aspects of yourself that you may try to ignore but actually hold the key to your genius.

Mary Morrissey
Founder of Brave Thinking™ Institute
August 2021

INTRODUCTION

Everyone has different parts of their personality. Some they like and some they wish would **just go away!**

So did I.

Making decisions was difficult. My life was confusing and embarrassing. Relationships and jobs were hard to keep. At times, I couldn't explain my behavior. I felt bad about myself and felt like something was wrong with me. Therapy didn't help, especially when I was misdiagnosed or overmedicated.

Finally, I found a clinician who knew about parts and downplayed the labels of mental illness. I felt further affirmed when Steven Spielberg produced the binge-watched TV series *United States of Tara* about a loving family, including a mom, Tara (played by Toni Collette), who has what was previously called multiple personalities. With love and humor, Hollywood brought to life what has often been portrayed as hateful, murderous, or schizophrenic.

Inspired and empowered, I became a therapist, a transformational life coach, and a consultant, helping clients, family members, and other medical and mental health professionals around the world to understand and love all the parts of themselves.

After many years of working with clients and through my personal research and experience, I found that sometimes, no matter how much we try—regardless of how smart we are, how much education, money, or privilege we have (and even when hypnosis hasn't worked)—there may be a part of ourselves that has the answer to what is keeping us stuck.

That is when the 3-step method described in this book may help, when everything else you have tried has not. Of course, this is a simplified version. At the very least, it will pique your curiosity and begin the process toward compassion and living your truth.

You may even discover your passion and your genius!

May you have compassion for others and all the parts of yourself—especially those you disagree with, don't like, don't understand, or fear—for a peaceful world.

Julie Kalmenson Lyons, LICSW

Just Say "Hi"™

is fun, playful, and what the world needs to

move forward with hope—Now!

Questions to Ponder:

Do you start a food plan or stop drinking, and everything is going great when out of nowhere you Just say, "Oh, F_ _ _ it?"

At times, does your GPS just not recognize your voice?

Do you find things in your closet you just don't remember buying?

Have you thought you were a procrastinator or a sabotager because you just could not complete a project?

Would you love to have a healthy relationship but just think you can't?

> ...maybe there is a part of you that **CAN!**

Julie Kalmenson Lyons, LICSW

☆

Using the 3-Step Method

Just Say "Hi"™

to help you identify, accept, and become loving and kind to **ALL** aspects of you.

Just Say "Hi"™

was
originally created to help people
with multiple personalities
(multiplicity)
or with the diagnosis dissociative
identity disorder (*DID*).

**But
every person
has unique parts of
themselves.**

Every person

has a multitude of characteristics,
skills, abilities, preferences,
moods, identity expressions,
sexualities,
and parts of themselves
they think
are wonderful

...and aspects or sides of
themselves they hide or wish
would just GO AWAY!

Multiplicity:

**an amazing kaleidoscope
of parts, or aspects of self,
with unique abilities,
physicalities, verbal skills,
sexualities, identity expressions,
mental diversities, and ethnicities that
make up a human being**

Mental Diversity

Unique coping styles and characteristics every person has to navigate life

Sometimes quite handy

...and sometimes they may keep you from feeling good about yourself or keep you stuck if you don't know what to do

What if you could look inside at the different parts of yourself?

Would you feel afraid?

It just might lead you to get unstuck and even to find your genius.

Some people are afraid to know everything about themselves.

Perhaps you are afraid to know
hidden parts of yourself
because you are worried
you might have symptoms
of a diagnosis.

Don't worry ... multiplicity is not bad.

You might discover a part of
yourself that has been holding
you back or an amazing part
that has the answer to a
problem or an
important secret that
can
get you unstuck.

But...

**what is the difference between
just having "parts"
and
the diagnosis
dissociative identity disorder?**

First, what is a diagnosis?

A **diagnosis**
is a term used to identify clusters of
measurable characteristics, behaviors,
or symptoms that appear in a certain
way and can be used to communicate
information with the goal of
helping people.

Used effectively,
a diagnosis can help
assess and treat a condition.

Learning about individual
coping styles can provide
an opportunity to decide
what works
and what doesn't.

The diagnosis
dissociative identity disorder (*DID*)*,
previously called multiple personality disorder,
key factors:

- having two or more significant or distinct personalities or identities
- profound and abrupt changes in mood or behavior
- time gaps you can't explain by just being forgetful

*For more information about the diagnosis, see Appendix for list of books.

Can a diagnosis be dangerous?

YES.

A diagnosis can be **dangerous if we think:**

- We know everything about the condition.
- Every person is the same in how it presents.
- People can't get well.
- We confuse one diagnosis with another.

People with a mental health diagnosis, especially dissociative identity disorder,
often struggle with addiction,
have been misdiagnosed,
disbelieved,
overmedicated,
hospitalized,
or remain hidden
and afraid.

It is very common
for people who live with
multiple personalities
to hide
to protect themselves
from being
judged.

Naturally, people would want to escape knowing about themselves to avoid possible stigma.

What people with symptoms of dissociative identity disorder (*DID*) or Multiplicity are NOT:

- They are *not* schizophrenic.
- They are *not* murderers.
- They are *not* bad, stuck, or incapable of having a successful life.
- They are *not crazy or insane*.

And many of them are high functioning.

One high-functioning adult client had an advanced degree and achieved financial success but felt stuck.

They wanted to have closer personal relationships, more intimacy with their partner, and to feel more confident in making friends. They had been ignoring aspects of themselves that had the answers.

After learning to listen inside, they were able to acknowledge parts of themselves that were afraid and needed encouragement—parts that they had not been aware of before.

Instead of scolding or shaming themselves because adults "should know how to do these things," they were able to learn the necessary skills and easily move forward and feel more fulfilled.

Another client felt like a failure because they could not stick with a diet and were unable to control their intake of food. They felt very discouraged and believed that part of them was a sabotager and uncooperative. They had been wishing for years, without any success, that they could just force that part of themselves to behave.

Finally, after investing in unsuccessful fad diets and restrictive eating, they agreed to start being curious about what that part of themselves was about and thanking it for getting their attention and uncovering something that was really important. That part of themselves actually held a secret that unlocked their truth and allowed them the freedom to finally be themselves and learn a new way of eating, naturally.

People can become
empowered by looking
inside at aspects of
themselves, learning new
skills
to feel better

...and thrive.

Finding out more about parts of yourself could give you the edge you need to really make a difference in the world...

How Just Say "Hi"™
Can Help
Everyone

Perhaps

you have been feeling stuck...

resisting necessary activities,
irritable, impatient with others,
or driving too fast,

or maybe you would simply like to
find your passion.

Just Say "Hi"™
can help you discover
parts of yourself to:

⭐ unlock your creativity

⭐ enhance your relationships

⭐ expand your possibilities

⭐ Just Say "Hi"™

can help you stop scolding or ignoring
parts of yourself that are interfering
in reaching your goals
or
achieving your dreams,
or
it can help you stop wishing that part of
you would
Just GO AWAY!

One friend was on her way to drop off her guitar for donation but decided to keep it when she heard about being curious about parts of herself. She had been scolding herself because she hadn't practiced playing music in a while, assuming she wasn't interested anymore. But instead, she thought, "Hmmm, maybe a part of me still wants to play the guitar when I have more time…"

Just Say "Hi"™

Can help you
stop discounting
unique aspects of yourself,
which may cause
anxiety
and even
violence—
directed inward,
hurting you,
or outward,
hurting others.

Another friend had been scolding himself for being "a procrastinator." But when he stopped shaming himself and started being curious about the part that just couldn't finish the project he was working on, he realized that there was another aspect of himself that had concerns about presenting the information to a group of people. If he finished the project, he would have to do something that scared him. He decided to be compassionate and kind to the part of himself that was afraid and cleared the way for completion of the project and a successful presentation.

Just Say "Hi"™

The 3-Step Method can
help you identify internal parts
by acknowledging them
and
welcoming them
to come
forward.

Yes...

Discovering parts of yourself beyond what you already know might be challenging.

Up until now,
you may have only wanted
to accept parts of you
that are funny, gifted, creative,
talented, and endearing.

Maybe

you thought it was best
to only appreciate your special qualities.
But
this is not your whole "self."

Accessing

aspects of you
that may have been ignored,
loathed,
or pushed aside
may really help you
reduce anxiety and
find greater
joy
and
freedom...

Freedom

to do big things,
to live your passion,
and find
your purpose...
Identifying internal parts
can give you a better relationship with
yourself and help you move forward,
beyond a pandemic or any other
circumstance, situation, or condition
that you think is **untenable.***

*absolutely unacceptable

Just Say "Hi"™

could help you
stop doing things to yourself that you
know are harmful
or help you
start doing something
you want to do
when *nothing else has worked.*

So...

when you feel stuck...

You can get unstuck.

Just Say "Hi"™

might just work!

 # The 3-Step Method

Just Say "Hi"™

Step One:

When you are feeling
UNCOMFORTABLE, CONFUSED, or
unable to find the answer...
or something outside of you is causing
you to feel stuck or upset,

Stop.

...Just pretend

you are talking to the most
precious little being*
that you can imagine...

Yaa, that gushy, mushy voice...

*or favorite little pet or plant

Julie Kalmenson Lyons, LICSW

Just Say **"Hi"**™

to your inside "self."

Just Say "Hi"™

and then
just listen...

But, what if I **just** can't do **Step I** and Just Say "Hi"™ **just** sounds ridiculous!?

That's OK.
Especially
if you are usually
self-sufficient,
successful,
and used to
solving problems yourself,

then
Step I may be difficult.

Or what if
you just can't stop yourself
from avoiding, pushing aside, or
ignoring the thing you think about
yourself
that is negative, evil, or
uncomfortable
and you just can't
make it go away?

...Then, maybe you just start
with Step Two.

Step Two

Just Be CURIOUS

Just Be Curious

Stop

whatever you are
saying to yourself,
whatever you are doing.

Just be CURIOUS...
then

ask the question *inside*...
"Is there a part of me that might need something?"

Just be CURIOUS...
And ask

"What would you like me to know?"

Or

"Is there a part that can help?"

...and then listen

...just try it

with an open mind...
and that gushy, mushy,
sweet, kind,
non-judgmental,
soft,
inquiring voice.

What if Step One and
Step Two
just don't work?

Then maybe you just
start with

Step Three

Step Three

Just Say Thank You

Just Say Thank You
to the thing that is in your way,
the thing you think
you can't stand
one more
minute.

Just Say Thank You

for being part of me—
for getting my attention
right now.

It may seem ridiculous
to Just Say Thank You
to a part of yourself
that you don't know is there
or that you don't like.
But ignoring it
just hasn't worked

so, Just try it...

When you
give recognition,
show appreciation,
pay attention,
and listen

... magic can happen.

It **Just** might be time to...

Just try this stuff!

There may be one area of your life or a situation
where everything you have tried

just doesn't work.

This is the time to

Just Say "Hi"™

...inside.

Just Say "Hi"™

will help you
learn about yourself,
acknowledge and
appreciate who you are,
And
if you have *DID*...
explore and gain insight
about your personalities
and know what to do.

Just Say "Hi"™

can also help people
have a better
understanding
of
Multiplicity
and
embrace
Mental Diversity.

It may feel uncomfortable
to consider having
parts of your personality that
you don't acknowledge or even
an **Internal Community...**

But...

What if an aspect of you has the answer?

Commonly Asked Questions

What do you mean by being stuck?

- Unable to take an action
- Jammed up on a creative project
- Confused about an important decision
- Trapped in an old habit
- Paralyzed with a sense of impending doom
- Sidestepping asking for help

What are examples of "parts"?

Aspects or facets of you that act and
feel differently at different times
(or often described as a side of you
that is childlike, a risk-taker, or the
mature one);
or you notice that you are better at a
particular task on a certain day
and not so good another, or you handle
a challenging situation you didn't know
you could, or
you feel like reading a book or not
or creative or not under different
circumstances

There is a part of me that seems to have disappeared. Where did it go?

Sometimes a part of us may be dormant, but usually it can still be accessed by asking another part for help, or it can be activated by using music, nature, or another person, place, or situation, especially if it is a part of you that is necessary for emergency purposes.

If I ask a part of myself what it needs to get unstuck, what happens next?

It depends on which part of you asks, what tone of voice you use, and if you decide to stop and listen. When you ask with kindness, love, and curiosity, another part of you may just answer.

What do I do if I don't agree with the answer? (My favorite question!)

A part of you probably will not agree.
This is another opportunity to be kind.
Ask for more information with
compassion, understanding, and a
desire for peace,
the way we might treat others in our
community who have different beliefs
than our own.

Thank You for Just Being Curious...

about Just Say "Hi"™

Julie Kalmenson Lyons, LICSW
Certified Life Mastery Consultant
Multiplicity Expert

Julie Lyons, LICSW, is a licensed clinical social worker, psychotherapist, certified life mastery consultant, gender specialist and multiplicity expert. Julie served on active duty in the U.S. Army during Desert Storm. Julie helps empower people to discover unique parts of themselves and find freedom to live their truth.

Different from therapy or life coaching alone, Julie's concierge program gives clients additional contact with a personal mentor. Clients have access to Julie's personal cell phone number and email, not only for emergency care but to share wins between sessions.

Julie has a warm, approachable, and professional style grounded in traditional theories, research, neuroscience, and personal experience, helping clients make quantum leaps where they previously felt stuck.

Individualized client contact is proven to have a direct effect on efficient, effective, long-term results.

Helping clients make quantum leaps where they previously felt stuck!

For information about Julie or her practice,
visit: https://www.justsay-hi.com/

Just Say "Hi!"™

Book Julie Kalmenson Lyons, LICSW
for a podcast or interview,
or to Speak at Your Next Event

To schedule an appointment or for

speaking, consulting, coaching, or to... Just Say
"Hi"™

email Julie at:

justsayhijulie@gmail.com

Every person wants to be loved...
especially our deepest self.

Listen inside today.

Just Say

"Hi"™

Endorsements

We really enjoyed getting to talk with other systems and found that really valuable. It felt welcoming for us."

Group participant, USA

"Our trust with you grows exponentially, and we are finding happiness in sharing with others about our neuro-diversity."

Group participant, USA

"What a relief to know there are other successful, multitalented people thriving by learning to use their internal diversity and uniqueness to produce creative projects and help others!"

Client, Japan

"Your presence in our lives has significantly changed us for the best. From the depths of our core, thank you."

Client, USA

"Shortly after I left my career of 40 years, I was diagnosed with cancer, and I decided to hire Julie as my Life Coach. I went through periods of depression, anger, and denial. Julie's knowledge, compassion, and creative method not only helped me get through my course of radiation therapy but helped me discover a new vocation."

WK (Cancer Survivor, Retired Chemical Engineer)

"You are a f---ing genius, Julie! Thank you for your help."

JW (Law Enforcement)

"A workable solution to what might seem like an untenable situation or circumstance in your life."

MB (VP of Operations)

"Julie's dedication as a mentor, teacher, and consultant has helped people all over the world learn to identify parts of themselves that used to cause them shame, embarrassment, and discomfort and now bring them success at school, work, and play."

EH (Owner/Creative Director, Ecommerce National Fashion Jewelry Brand)

"Julie's 3-step method can be used to give you an edge in successfully moving forward in your life. From entrepreneurs to educators, entertainment personalities to medical professionals, learning how to welcome aspects of ourselves and others we do not understand helps bring peace in any situation and understanding in a world that really needs it right now."

JE (Director, International Food Chain)

Glossary

Personality: An individual's general character, makeup, disposition, and temperament, including behaviors, attributes, or traits

Part: A separate identity, persona, aspect, or facet of a person with distinct differences from two or more others in one person

System: An individual who has identified separate, distinct personalities within themselves, often referred to as "alters"

Mental Diversity: A rainbow of unique thinking patterns and coping styles affecting thoughts, feelings, and behaviors used to navigate life

Alter: A distinctly different part of one's personality other than the one they were born with, usually in the case of someone who has multiple personalities or the diagnosis of dissociative identity disorder, which may be visibly apparent and include different gender, sexuality, ethnicity, abilities, likes and dislikes, verbal or visual skills, age, voice qualities, memories, and general knowledge

Dissociative Identity Disorder (*DID*): Previously called multiple personality disorder; having two or more significant or distinct personalities or identities evidenced by profound and abrupt changes in mood or behavior, time gaps unexplainable by common forgetfulness as the result of severe trauma (For a full definition and information, see Appendix.)

Multiplicity: An amazing kaleidoscope of parts, or aspects of self, with unique abilities, physicalities, verbal skills, sexualities, identity expressions, mental diversities, and ethnicities that make up a human being

Host: The main part of the personality that is most predominant, not always the one the person was born with

Schizophrenic: Appearing to have delusions, hallucinations, paranoia, and disorganized thought, speech, and/or behavior patterns; pertaining to the mental disorder schizophrenia

Mental Disorder: A condition characterized by the occurrence of a specific group of symptoms, behaviors, and characteristics as defined by the diagnostic and statistical manual of mental disorders (DSM-V) published by the American Psychiatric Association

Aspects: Facets or parts of the self

Personas: Used to describe aspects, alters, or parts of self; historically used to describe the personality one shows in public or the mask one wears in society, hiding their true self (referred to by the Swiss psychologist Carl Jung); also used to describe fictional characters or product users in marketing

Dissociation: Frequent or prolonged occurrences of disconnection with one's main personality, surroundings, or memory (Some forms of dissociation from reality are common, such as while doing a monotonous activity like driving or walking a daily route or watching television and not noticing someone walk by.)

Appendix:

**For more information on
dissociative identity disorder**

Crisis Hotlines:

https://did-research.org/resources/hotlines

General Clinical Information:

https://did-research.org/

Mental Health Hotlines

- US: 1-630-482-9696 (Suicide Prevention Services of America and Suicide Prevention Lifeline; also has hotlines specifically for suicide prevention at 1-800-273-8255 (1-800-273-TALK) and 1-800-784-2433 (1-800-SUICIDE) as well as a hotline for Spanish speakers at 1-888-628-9454 and for individuals who are d/Deaf or hard of hearing at 1-800-799-4889; also allows chat; accepts youth, LGBT individuals, Native Americans, veterans, and survivors of suicide attempts)

- US: Suicide Hotlines by State

- US: Peer Support "Warmlines" by State

- US and Canada: Text 741741 (US) / 686868 (Canada) (Crisis Text Line; also accepts messages through Facebook messenger at facebook.com/crisistextline; connects individuals to trained volunteers; LGBT friendly)

- UK and ROI: 116-123 (Samaritans; free to call; also accepts emails to jo@samaritans.org (UK) or jo@samaritans.ie (ROI); has a Welsh language line at 0808-164-0123 that›s open evenings into the early morning; accepts youth)

- UK: 01708-765200 (SupportLine; also accepts emails to info@supportline.org.uk; for youth and adults, including survivors of abuse and individuals from marginalized communities)

- UK: 0300-304-7000 (SANEline; open from 4.30pm to 10.30pm; for anyone 16+ who is in crisis and affected by mental illness, including loved ones and caregivers; has a text service for requests for information or other non-crisis needs)

- Australia: 13 11 14 (Lifeline; available 24/7; available to d/Deaf, hard-of-hearing, or speech-impaired individuals through the National Relay Service (TTY: 133 677; Speak and Listen: 1300 555 727); translation available through 131 450; online crisis chat also available from 7pm to midnight; trial text services also available at 0477 13 11 14 from 5pm to 9pm; accepts all ages, genders, sexualities, ethnicities, and religions)

- **Australia:** Mental Health Crisis Lines by Region
- **International:** Befrienders Worldwide Hotlines
- **International:** Hotlines by Country
- **International:** Suicide Hotlines by Country
- **International:** Online Crisis Chats
- **International:** Crisis Centers and Hotlines by Country and Online Resources

**For More information on
dissociative identity disorder**

General Clinical Information:
https://did-research.org/

Books on Parts and Multiplicity:

-United We Stand: A Book for People with Multiple
Personalities
By Eliana Gil, PhD

-No Bad Parts: Healing Trauma & Restoring
Wholeness with the Internal Family Systems Model
By Richard C. Schwartz, PHD, foreword
by Alanis Morissette

-YOU ARE THE ONE YOU'VE BEEN WAITING
FOR: Bringing Courageous Love to Intimate
Relationships
By Richard C. Schwartz

There is always a part of you
that has the answer.